# Welcome!

One of the most important yet hardest parts of
learning anything new is applying what you learn.
This is also true for skills gained from dialectical
behavior therapy (DBT)! Taking the DBT skills
you've learned in a skills group (or through self-
help books, videos, or cards) and using them in
your real life can be tricky. There are dozens of
skills and tons of acronyms, so how are you supposed to remember everything? That's where this
deck comes in.

  *DBT Cards for Coping Skills* includes 125 com-
pact, portable cards with bite-sized info about DBT
skills. Most cards cover the material taught in Dr.
Marsha M. Linehan's original skills book: *DBT Skills
Training Handouts and Worksheets*, second edition.
Others provide some new ideas for DBT-inspired
coping. The cards (listed on pages 27 to 31 of this
booklet) are designed to help you learn, remember,
and practice DBT skills in your everyday life.

## How to Use This Deck

DBT skills are helpful for improving mental health but only if you use them regularly. There are tons of ways this deck can support you. Here are some ideas:

- Read through all the cards to learn the DBT skills or to refresh your memory.
- Use the cards like traditional flash cards to help you study and memorize DBT skills.
- Pick a card at random each day and practice that skill at least once.
- Put favorite cards in your Distress Tolerance Kit (Card 56).
- Have your therapist select a card for you to practice each week.
- Lay cards out on a table, grouping them together to create Cope Ahead (Card 94) plans. Take a photo to help you remember.
- Share cards with a loved one so they can practice new skills along with you or help you in crisis.
- Combine any or all of the above!

No DBT skill will work for you every time you use it, but every skill is useful in the right circumstance. It's important to give every skill a chance, practicing each one a few times. If you use this deck in its entirety, you'll learn which skills you like best. You'll also learn which skills work well together, in what order, and for which emotions. Eventually, you'll start using skills without even thinking about it! That's when the life-changing power of DBT really happens.

This expertise takes time and practice. It also helps to have some deeper understanding of DBT principles. This booklet provides that foundational knowledge, as well as some basic information about the cards. While the cards are meant to stand alone, reading this booklet (and referring to it as needed) will ground your use of the skills.

# What Is DBT? Can It Help Me?

DBT is a specific type of cognitive behavioral therapy (CBT), a group of therapies based on the idea that your emotions, thoughts, and behaviors are interconnected and influence one another. CBT theory states that by changing one part of this three-part "triangle" system, you naturally change other parts.

DBT is a particularly behavioral form of CBT. It focuses on changing problematic behaviors in order to help people reduce emotional suffering. It also teaches many coping skills to help. DBT differs from traditional CBT, however, in that it also emphasizes mindfulness, dialectics, and some acceptance-based principles inspired by Zen Buddhism (more on these parts later!).

DBT is a powerful and complex psychotherapy. Decades of research show that DBT helps people with borderline personality disorder (BPD). It's also an effective treatment for PTSD, ADHD, substance use disorders, some eating disorders, and more. Most of this research studies "comprehensive DBT." Comprehensive DBT always includes four modes of treatment: weekly individual DBT therapy, a weekly DBT skills group, as-needed phone coaching calls with a DBT therapist between sessions, and weekly DBT consultation team meetings (for the therapist, not the client).

DBT skills are just one aspect of comprehensive DBT. Practicing these skills can be helpful for anyone trying to improve their mental health, no matter their age, culture, or unique struggles. That's because DBT skills are life skills. They're particularly useful for highly sensitive people or people who feel emotions intensely.

Beyond providing the four modes of treatment, DBT therapists follow certain guidelines and theories that are unique to DBT. While most of these apply to the therapist specifically, there are a few that I often share with my clients to help them get the most out of therapy. Even if you only want to learn DBT skills, understanding these will likely help you, too. Let's dive in.

## DBT's Primary Goal

DBT's main goal is helping people build a "Life Worth Living"—the life each person would personally find most joyful and fulfilling. All DBT skills and practices turn back to this question: In this moment, is what you're doing taking you closer to or further away from your Life Worth Living?

Sometimes building your ideal life involves setting goals, taking action toward those goals, and problem-solving to overcome obstacles. Sometimes it involves practicing mindfulness, simply being present in the moment, and enjoying (or at least tolerating) what your life already entails. Usually, you have to jump back and forth between these (see Card 11). This dance is one of the main features of DBT: balancing acceptance and change.

## Dialectics

The balance of acceptance and change is one of the core dialectical tensions of DBT. Dialectics (the *D* in DBT!) is a philosophy and way of thinking that centers on the idea that two seemingly opposite things can be true at the same time.

When you get very upset, it's likely that you start thinking in more all-or-nothing or extreme ways. That's human! For folks who feel emotions intensely, however, this human tendency can cause a lot of problems. If you're constantly changing moods, your thoughts are likely to follow suit, which can make it difficult to understand yourself, maintain stable relationships, or make life decisions.

Increasing your ability to find the middle-ground truth between extremes is another major goal of DBT. Learning to harmonize acceptance and change is one of the most difficult and most important dialectics to master as you work toward emotional wellness.

That's because, in DBT, we view acceptance and change as our only options for dealing with problems in life. Specifically, we say there are always four—and only four—options:

1. Change our situation: If we can solve the problem and change the situation, then the painful emotions caused by the problem change, too.

2. Change our reactions to the situation: We can change how we think about or respond to a painful situation, which can change how we feel (even if we can't fix a problem).

3. Accept our situation: If we can fully acknowledge a problem and tolerate our emotional pain, even if we don't approve of or like it, we can decrease our suffering.

4. Stay miserable (or make things worse): If we don't like the sound of any of the other options, we can always choose to practice no skills and continue to suffer.

# The Four Skills Modules

If you looked at the options on the previous page and didn't understand how you're possibly supposed to do some of them, don't worry! That's where DBT skills come in. There are dozens of DBT skills for the first three options, spread across four modules (each with its own unique color in this deck):

**Mindfulness (green cards):** Skills for improving attention and increasing wisdom and peace. By practicing being in the present moment, exactly as it is, you can learn to live a more embodied, liberated, and authentic life.

**Emotion Regulation (blue cards):** Skills for understanding, feeling, using, and changing emotions. This module will help you better relate to and work with your emotional experiences in specific moments while increasing your overall emotional resilience.

**Distress Tolerance (purple cards):** Skills for coping with the most painful experiences in life. When you can't change reality or change how you feel about it, you can use these skills to survive emotional pain without acting impulsively, dissociating, or suppressing.

**Interpersonal Effectiveness (orange cards):** Skills for improving communication and relationships. This module will teach you skills for asserting yourself and saying no while effectively balancing your needs with others' needs.

Everyone struggles in these four areas from time to time. That's why DBT skills are life skills. Mindfulness and Distress Tolerance skills are typically acceptance-oriented, while Emotion Regulation and Interpersonal Effectiveness skills are typically change-oriented. Weaving the skills together creates the most emotional transformation.

# How Do I Know Which Skills to Use and When?

There are many DBT skills. Your preferences and needs are unique to you, but there are some general guidelines that apply to most people when trying to decide which skills to use and when.

Think about your emotions as ranging in intensity on a scale of 0 (not feeling it at all) to 10 (feeling it the most you possibly can). You'll be using Mindfulness (Cards 1 to 15) at all emotional levels as a part of practicing other DBT skills. But when you're just starting out, it's helpful to practice Mindfulness skills (or any new skill) at emotional intensities under 5.

When your emotions are higher (often somewhere between 7 and 10 on your intensity scale), you're more likely to reach your "skills breakdown point." This is when you feel totally overwhelmed and unable to think clearly—and that's your cue to use Crisis Survival skills (Cards 16 to 46) until your emotional intensity and overwhelm decrease.

When your emotions are lower (often 6 or below), your emotions are less likely to "overload" you. Whenever you're able to access Wise Mind

(Cards 9 and 10), you can use any skill that would be effective for you. If you're facing a specific problem, it may be useful to use Emotion Regulation (Cards 60 to 103) and Interpersonal Effectiveness (Cards 104 to 122). If you can't change a situation that's causing you emotional pain, all Distress Tolerance skills may still be necessary, particularly the Acceptance skills (Cards 47 to 53). If what you're doing isn't working, read pages 19 to 22 in this booklet and Card 124!

When you're vulnerable, your skills breakdown point may be triggered at lower intensities than normal for you. As your emotional resilience improves, your skills breakdown point will be triggered at higher and higher intensities.

Finally, if you ever feel like you're somehow below a 0 or off the scale entirely, like you're numb or dissociated or totally burned-out, you'll likely benefit from using skills that regulate your nervous system and care for your physical body (see Cards 19 to 23, 32 to 38, and 95 to 102).

## How DBT Views Emotions

Perhaps it's useful to say at this point that emotion regulation is not about eliminating emotions. Many people come to DBT because they're in a lot of emotional pain. If this is you, it may feel like emotions are "driving the car" of your life, deciding where you're going and when. DBT skills are designed to help you take the wheel. But you don't want to kick emotions out of the car entirely! You want to consider them when making decisions about where to go. That's because your emotions are designed to help you.

Humans evolved emotions as one way to make sense of our world and our experiences. Emotions can act like red, green, and beige flags. They get your attention and give you information about what you like and dislike.

Emotions can protect and assist you. They make you feel like doing things. These "action urges" can feel like physical sensations—skin-crawling that makes you flinch in disgust, warmth in your face that makes you smile with gratitude, or agitation in your muscles that makes you run away in fear.

Emotions can also communicate with and influence other people. For example, if you cry when sad, it may evoke supportive actions in others, like someone offering a hug or a tissue.

In these ways, emotions support building your Life Worth Living. If you constantly ignore or suppress emotions, they can't help you. Therefore, Emotion Regulation skills teach us to understand, feel, and respect our emotions—not just stop or change them. DBT skills can cause certain people to feel *more* painful emotions at first, as DBT helps people to stop avoiding their emotional experiences. But with practice and time, feeling and working with your emotions gets easier. The DBT skills will help you view your emotions as superpowers rather than as burdens.

# Emotions: Always Valid, Not Always Justified

Because emotions are so helpful for surviving and thriving, we can be supersensitive to them. We naturally (and sometimes subconsciously) make emotional connections and remember them for a long time. While this emotional wiring can help us avoid harmful people, places, or behaviors, it also can cause problems when we don't stay mindful of where our emotions are coming from.

Emotions can be triggered by many things. Sometimes emotions are prompted by external events, and other times they are prompted by faulty beliefs. Emotions themselves, then, can't be inherently trusted as facts. To be clear: All emotions are real, meaning that you're really feeling them. And all emotions make sense and are valid, meaning that *something* triggered them. But not all emotions are caused by proven facts or accurate interpretations of what's happening.

In DBT, we use the terms "justified" and "unjustified" when differentiating between emotional reactions. If an emotion is prompted by a situation or an actual event, it is justified and "fits the facts." If an emotion is prompted (or intensified) by inaccurate thoughts, it is unjustified and does not fit the facts. We use the Check the Facts skill (Card 73) to explore and determine whether an emotion is unjustified or justified.

Remember, all emotions are valid and understandable. There's always a cause for your emotions. So, determining that your emotion is unjustified does not mean it's OK to invalidate or judge yourself and the emotion. But knowing whether your emotion fits the facts matters because it influences how to respond to that emotion most effectively.

One additional distinction that's important for deciding how to respond to emotions is whether the emotion is "effective" for you to act on.

In DBT, we say an emotion is effective if its action urge (i.e., what the emotion makes you want to do) would make you do things that would help you toward your Life Worth Living. An emotion is "ineffective" if acting on its action urge would hurt you, hinder your progress toward your goals, or otherwise cause you problems worse than its benefits.

You get to decide what is most effective for you—not me, not your therapist, not your friend, just you. Of course, sometimes intense emotions can make us really willful—we may get stubborn about using skills, we may have urges to give up, we may know what's "right" to do but kind of ignore it, stomp our feet, or lift our noses up at it. Practicing Willingness (Card 48), the skill of doing what's needed in this moment, will be important.

## Some Final Words

Being willing, using new skills, and building a Life Worth Living can be very hard at times. It can be useful to remember the "DBT Assumptions."

In DBT, we believe these statements to be true:

- Everything is caused. Each moment, built upon the last moment, could be no other way.
- In each moment, we are all doing the best we possibly can.
- We all want to improve, and we all need to do better and try harder to change.
- Compassionately figuring out the causes of our behaviors is more effective than judging or blaming.

Self-improvement takes time and effort. If you're here, trying, that's amazing. Remember, you want to do better and you're doing the best you can.

If you find that you're trying your best to use the skills, but you keep struggling or not getting the results you want, the following troubleshooting guides may be helpful.

# Troubleshoot: When Emotion Regulation Skills Aren't Working

1. **Are you emotionally vulnerable or in a really bad mood?**

   Check in with your physical health, and resolve any issues accordingly, likely with PLEASES (Cards 95 to 101) or Self-Soothing (Cards 32 to 38).

2. **Are you using the skills effectively?**

   Identify the specific skills you've been trying to use. Double-check the instructions of those skills. Ask a therapist or trusted friend for help.

3. **Are unwanted emotions being reinforced by something?**

   Even if the emotions are painful, identify what they are giving you that's "positive." Do they feel good in some way, or are they getting you something else you want? Self-Validate (Card 114); let yourself feel your emotion before trying to change it. Practice Pros and Cons (Card 18) of using skills or acting in Emotion Mind (Card 9). Problem-Solve (Card 78) how to get what feels good using your skills. Assert your needs to others directly (see Cards 107 to 109).

4.  **Are you getting impatient or willful?**
    Remember that change takes time. Practice Radical Acceptance (Card 47) and Crisis Survival skills as needed (Cards 16 to 46).

5.  **Are you emotionally overwhelmed?**
    Use TIPP (Cards 19 to 23) and other Crisis Survival skills (Cards 16 to 46) until your emotion decreases or until you can access Wise Mind (Card 9).

6.  **Are emotion "myths" getting in your way?**
    Remember the "facts" about emotions (see booklet pages 13 to 17 and Card 60). Challenge any myths or Cognitive Distortions (Card 75) you're thinking. Describe your emotion and the situation Nonjudgmentally (Card 6).

# Troubleshoot: When Interpersonal Effectiveness Skills Aren't Working

1.  **Are you using effective skills effectively?**
    Identify the specific skills you've been trying to use. Double-check the instructions of those skills. Ask a therapist or trusted friend for help.

2.  **Have you fully and honestly identified what you want?**
    Clarify Interpersonal Goals (Card 106). Practice Opposite Action (Card 76) to shame or fear caused by thoughts like, "You don't deserve to say no or to ask for what you want."

3.  **Are short-term desires getting in the way of long-term goals?**
    Confirm the ranking of your interpersonal goals. Practice Wise Mind (Card 10) about how to approach the situation. Use Pros and Cons (Card 18), or practice Opposite Action (Card 76) to action urges caused by Emotion Mind (Card 9).

4. **Are you emotionally overwhelmed?**
   Use Crisis Survival skills (Cards 16 to 46),
   including TIPP (Cards 19 to 23), until your
   emotion decreases to a point when you can
   communicate in a Wise Mind (Card 9) way.

5. **Are judgments/myths getting in your way?**
   Remember the Facts about Relationships/
   Communication (Card 104). Challenge any
   myths or Cognitive Distortions (Card 75) you're
   thinking about. Use Coping Statements for
   People Pleasers (Card 121). Dialectically validate
   both you and the other person (see Cards 110 to
   111 and 113 to 114).

6. **Is the environment just too powerful?**
   Radically Accept (Card 47) your current reality
   and limitations. Find a powerful ally who can
   advocate on your behalf. Find community that
   can validate your experience. Problem-Solve
   (Card 78) other ways to get what you want.

## Want More Support While Learning DBT Skills?

- Read *Self-Directed DBT Skills: A 3-Month DBT Workbook* by Drs. Kiki Fehling and Elliot Weiner (published by Zeitgeist, 2023).

- Find a certified expert DBT therapist through the DBT-Linehan Board of Certification at dbt-lbc.org.

- Find an intensively trained DBT therapist through Behavioral Tech Institute at behavioraltech.org/find-a-therapist-app.

- Watch YouTube videos on the @dbtkiki, @DBTRU, and @dbtsandiego channels.

- Follow DBT-related content creators on social media, such as @dbtexchange, @lenanicodemustherapy, @onlinedbtskills, and @dbtselfhelpsite.

- Listen to podcasts: *The Skillful Podcast* from the Bay Area DBT & Couples Counseling Center, *To Hell and Back* with Charles Swenson, and *Therapists in the Wild* with Drs. Molly St. Denis and Liza Pincus.

- Join online communities, such as DBT Self Help on Reddit (reddit.com/r/dbtselfhelp).

# Resources and References

All DBT skills information used in this deck comes from Dr. Marsha M. Linehan's books:

*DBT Skills Training Handouts and Worksheets*, second edition. New York: Guilford Press, 2014.

*DBT Skills Training Manual*, second edition. New York: Guilford Press, 2014.

Other resources were consulted for skills information, including:

Adams-Clark, Alexis A., Xi Yang, Monika N. Lind, Christina Gamache Martin, and Maureen Zalewski. "I'M SORRY: A New DBT Skill for Effective Apology." *DBT Bulletin* 6, no. 1 (2022): 29–33.

Brook, Amara, Rachel Leah Kraus, Charity Chaney, and Charles Swenson. "Increasing Effectiveness of DBT for Autistic Adults." Presented at the 28th Annual ISITDBT Conference, Seattle, WA, November 2023.

Brown, Brené. "Dare to Lead List of Values." Accessed February 3, 2024. https://brenebrown.com/resources/dare-to-lead-list-of-values.

Clear, James. "Core Values List." Accessed February 3, 2024. https://jamesclear.com/core-values.

**The following are references for other information included in this deck.**

Ben-Porath, Denise, Florencia Duthu, Tana Luo, Fragiskos Gonidakis, Emilio J. Compte, and Lucene Wisniewski. "Dialectical Behavioral Therapy: An Update and Review of the Existing Treatment Models Adapted for Adults with Eating Disorders." *Eating Disorders* 28, no. 2 (March–April 2020): 101–121. doi: 10.1080/10640266.2020.1723371.

Fleming, Andrew P., Robert J. McMahon, Lyndsey R. Moran, A. Paige Peterson, and Anthony Dreessen. "Pilot Randomized Controlled Trial of Dialectical Behavior Therapy Group Skills Training for ADHD among College Students." *Journal of Attention Disorders* 19, no. 3 (May 2014): 260–271. doi.org/10.1177/1087054714535951.

Haktanir, Abdulkadir, and Karisse A. Callender. "Meta-Analysis of Dialectical Behavior Therapy (DBT) for Treating Substance Use." *Research on Education and Psychology* 4 (Special Issue) (April 2020): 74–87. epublications.marquette.edu/edu_fac/598.

Harned, Melanie S., Kathryn E. Korslund, and Marsha M. Linehan. "A Pilot Randomized Controlled Trial of Dialectical Behavior Therapy with and without the Dialectical Behavior Therapy Prolonged Exposure Protocol for Suicidal and Self-Injuring Women with Borderline Personality Disorder and PTSD." *Behaviour Research and Therapy* 55 (April 2014): 7–17. doi: 10.1016/j.brat.2014.01.008.

Panos, Patrick T., John W. Jackson, Omar Hasan, and Angelea Panos. "Meta-Analysis and Systematic Review Assessing the Efficacy of Dialectical Behavior Therapy (DBT)." *Research on Social Work Practice* 24, no. 2 (March 2014): 213–223. doi: 10.1177/1049731513503047.

Valentine, Sarah E., Sarah M. Bankoff, Renée M. Poulin, Esther B. Reidler, and David W. Pantalone. "The Use of Dialectical Behavior Therapy Skills Training as Stand-Alone Treatment: A Systematic Review of the Treatment Outcome Literature." *Journal of Clinical Psychology* 71, no. 1 (January 2015): 1–20. doi: 10.1002/jclp.22114.

## Cards in This Deck

For your reference, the next few pages contain a list of all the cards in this deck. Most cards cover skills or concepts that come directly from DBT's treatment manuals. Some cards, identified with an asterisk below, offer adaptations or new ideas that can help you practice the traditional DBT skills.

Some cards provide tips on how to practice certain DBT skills in various situations. Keep in mind that these cards are simply educational and that not every suggestion will be relevant to you. Before practicing any specific skill, it's important to consider your emotions, health, and needs, ideally with a therapist or other supportive professional.

## Mindfulness

1. The "What" Skills
2. Observe
3. Describe
4. Participate
5. The "How" Skills
6. Nonjudgmentally
7. One-mindfully
8. Effectively
9. Wise Mind
10. Wise Mind Practices
11. Skillful Means
12. Observing the Breath
13. Do a Body Scan
14. External Mindfulness Ideas*
15. Loving-Kindness

## Distress Tolerance

16. Crisis Survival Skills
17. STOP
18. Pros and Cons
19. TIPP
20. Tip Your Temperature (TIPP)
21. Intense Exercise (TIPP)
22. Paced Breathing (TIPP)
23. Paired Muscle Relaxation (TIPP)
24. ACCEPTS
25. Activities (ACCEPTS)
26. Contributing (ACCEPTS)
27. Comparisons (ACCEPTS)
28. Emotions (ACCEPTS)
29. Pushing Away (ACCEPTS)
30. Thoughts (ACCEPTS)
31. Sensations (ACCEPTS)
32. Self-Soothing
33. Vision
34. Hearing
35. Smell
36. Taste

## Emotion Regulation

# About the Author

 **Kiki Fehling, PhD, DBT-LBC,** is a licensed psychologist, writer, speaker, and expert in dialectical behavior therapy (DBT). They specialize in borderline personality disorder, self-harm and suicide, trauma, and LGBTQ+ mental health. After witnessing the power of DBT skills in her own life and the lives of her clients, Kiki developed a passion for sharing those skills with as many people as possible. She co-authored the book *Self-Directed DBT Skills*, writes for *Psychology Today* and other publications, and shares mental health tips through her @dbtkiki social media accounts. Kiki is immensely thankful to Clara, Tahra, Carol, Dan, Elliot, and all her clients and followers who have made her a better person and DBT teacher.